THE
MAKER'S GUIDE
TO BUILDING
ROBOTS

EVERYTHING YOU NEED TO KNOW
TO BUILD YOUR OWN FROM SCRATCH

RAÚL LAPEIRA & ANDREU MARSAL
ILLUSTRATED BY ALEJANDRA MORENILLA

Translated by Allie Hauptman

Sky Pony Press
New York

Library of Congress Cataloging-in-Publication Data is available on file.

Cover design by Daniel Brount
Cover illustrations by Alejandra Morenilla

Print ISBN: 978-1-5107-4428-8
Ebook ISBN: 978-1-5107-4427-1

Printed in the United States of America

CONTENTS

— III —

Turn on your television and there they are! They're starring in movies; they make cakes decorated with the *Hearthstone* logo; they tell you if it's going to rain or if you've closed the fridge, or they quietly clean your house...

Robots are everywhere! But you know what? We love this invasion. Bit by bit, these "bugs" have become our friends. Now we need to get to know them, to learn how they work and how to manage them. You'll find all this and much more in this book. You'll even learn how to build your own robot. Great plan, right?

Quick! Find your favorite seat and get comfortable, turn the page, and say hi to our robots!

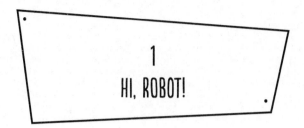

1
HI, ROBOT!

But . . . what is a robot?

Nothing would please us more than to present to you a single robot who would explain to you in a flash how it works. "Hi, humanoid," he would say to you in a mechanical voice as he stiffly extended his friendly hand. (As we will see, this and much more is possible today.) The truth is, if this were the case, if only one kind of robot existed, this would be a very boring book. We are telling you right now that robotics is very **FUN** and **EXCITING**. You'll see!

Depending whom you ask, you'll get different definitions of what a robot is; a ton of debate surrounds what constitutes a robot. Don't think the experts on this subject spend all our time throwing cables and electronic circuits at each other's heads over these questions; it's just that we have different opinions. For example, some define a robot as a mechanism; others, as a computer program. Some believe a robot can be defined as both of these things. For others, a robot must be constructed in the form of a living being. It's dizzying!

This mess might seem silly, but it can cause a lot of problems when it comes time to exchange information and ideas while studying robotics.

The one thing everyone agrees on is what defines a virtual robot: a computer program, without physical form, that does work that can be considered intelligent and that is capable of working on its own, for example, to play *League of Legends*, *Counter-Strike*, and other video games. To make something like this, you need to write a code: a series of lines written in programming language. Google "matrix," click on "images," and you will see these lines! Not all robots are like this, clearly; "lifelike" ones are built with cables and electronic circuits.

If we take all these facts into account and consider practical and humble household appliances, we find that despite the many functions they have, they can't be defined as robots. In this book, we will see that we will refer to a Vitamix as a robot; however, many of us who special-ize in robotics do not consider it to be one, even though we love the smoothies it makes! Sorry, Vitamix...

Therefore, to summarize, a simple and clear definition of robot would be this: "a logical or physical autonomous machine," or, for example, saying that your ball moves without your direct control. And how do you do this?

Thanks to hardware (electronic plates, motors, batteries, housing) and to software (programming, logic).

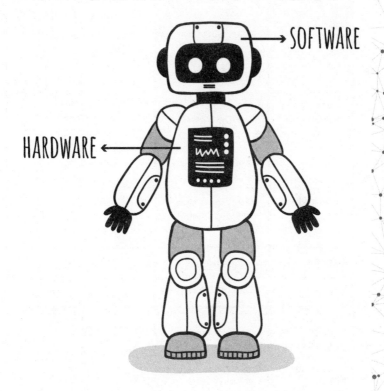

There are actually more robots designed with software than hardware. In the grid on the next page, we will show you some examples so you can see that the great and important friendship between software and hardware is fundamental to create certain types of robots.

Autonomous Bug/Robot	What it does	Proportion of software (approx.)	Proportion of hardware (approx.)
Aimbot	Helps you find targets in multiplayer shooter games	100%	0%
Chess Videogame	Applies an algorithm (a set of rules) that creates a good opponent for you to play against	100%	0%
Self-driving Car	Navigates roads without a driver	70%	30%
SpaceX Reusable Rocket	Takes off, travels in space, and lands, all autonomously	50%	50%
Traditional Industrial Arm	Welds cars or moves weights	20%	80%
Kitchen Robot	Performs certain cooking tasks and processes foods	5%	95%

Think about this rocket that travels to space, returns to Earth, and lands. Amazing! Though rockets have existed for a hundred years, we only now have sufficient technology to create one that lands autonomously. Can you call this type of space vehicle a robot? Many people don't believe so, but is it less intelligent than an industrial arm? Does it have fewer motors or fewer lines of code?

As we outlined in the table, software helps create a more intelligent robot, a more "logical brain." It is not surprising that this is the most innovative area of robotics.

Rap and Circuits

Maybe you're thinking that rockets and intelligence have as little to do with each other as a grasshopper and a

Bengal tiger. That they are as different as creating a rap song, a poem, a movie script, or an opera.

Every person has their own idea of what is or isn't "intelligence." For example, would you say that someone who can't write a good poem isn't intelligent? Or on the contrary, that the person who wrote the script for the *Transformers* movie has a stratospheric intellect?

While discussing human intelligence is a delicate topic, in robotics there's no danger that a line follower (a very simple robot that will follow any black line drawn on the floor) will be hurt if you said he wasn't very clever. The intelligence of a robot can range from something as basic as following a black line to diagnosing a health problem by reviewing symptoms. All of this is intelligence. Yes, of course, but getting a rocket to land autonomously requires an extra boost, don't you think?

Good Robots and Lying Robots

Speaking of intelligence, let us present one of our favorite science fiction writers, Isaac Asimov.

Though it sounds strange, literature has always played an important role in robotics. In his collection of stories, *I, Robot,* Asimov outlines the "three laws of robotics," which in theory define the behavior of a robot.

1. A robot should never harm a human, or, by its inaction, allow a human to be harmed.

2. A robot should obey the orders given to it by a human, unless these orders are in conflict with the first law.
3. A robot should protect its own existence, as long as this protection is not in conflict with the first or second law.

Of course, real robots are not programmed with these laws. And, of course, robots like the automated Predator plane from the United States Army—war planes—do not have rules like this in their code.

As we said, robotics and science fiction go hand in hand. This literary genre plays with physics, biology, and chemistry, and invents impossible stories about imaginary futures that enthrall a great number of readers.

Something very curious has happened with respect to robotics: reality has imitated these stories, but it has also surpassed them. Every year, we see new robots do new things. Robotics greatly exceeds what the authors and screenwriters of the 1950s and 1960s could have ever imagined.

In this era, movies did not employ CGI (computer generated images). If the plot of a movie required a robot, a human wore a robot costume, and everyone was happy. The costume would be made from metal or plastic pieces, almost like a suit of armor from the Middle Ages. The actor would have to move stiffly, almost like a penguin.

Take for instance C-3PO, the android from Star Wars. At the beginning of the series, he did not have much mobility, and it remained that way in later movies. The filmmakers were thoughtful and maintained this characteristic in all the following movies. It became something fans of C-3PO love about him.

The animated figure for Yoda was very convincing. He really looked like a living being, but in reality was nothing more than a bunch of motors and cables that created his movements. When the prequel (the story that preceded the original trilogy) premiered, Yoda was shown doing jumps worthy of an Olympic gymnast, which surprised the public, but it really wasn't all that strange; Yoda was much younger in this trilogy. If instead of showing Yoda bouncing around, C-3PO had been shown juggling, many people would have stormed out of the theater.

From a Duck with a Belly to 3D: Robots Throughout History

Let's take a giant leap back in time to Ancient Greece. Here we'll find what are considered some of the first prototypes for robots, as described in their mythology. They talk about mechanical beings or statues made in the form of humans. Yes, no one can beat the Greeks for their imagination.

It is not until the eighteenth century that the first robot, known as the "Canard Digérateur" (duck with a digestive apparatus) is seen in historical documents. The little animal in question simulates eating, does its business, and moves around a little. Its inventor was Jaques de Vaucanson, and it was such a significant invention that the famous philosopher Voltaire said about him:

"If it weren't for the voice of le Maure and Vaucanson's duck, you would have nothing to remind you of the glory of France." Tragically, Vaucanson's duck was lost in a fire centuries ago. We do not know if it quacked, and there are no photos or original drawings that we can use to estimate his size. Nevertheless, there are sufficient historical references to confirm its existence.

The lost duck competes with the Turk, dated at 1770, for the first robot ever made. It looked like a human, and it was also capable of playing a game of chess. The creator of this marvelous trick was the Hungarian Wolfgang von Kempelen. In reality, this contraption didn't move any of its fake fingers on its own, and it was actually a hoax, a lie worthy of a movie.

The Turk had a compartment for a person to fit in, but from the outside it looked as though the robot was playing chess. This invention tricked tons of people for more than eighty years.

Coming back to reality, some people believe that the first robot was in fact a chess player, but in this case, without the extra help that the Turk had. It was built in 1912 by Torres de Quevedo.

Torres de Quevedo was a major genius. He invented a machine that did mathematical calculations, another that tested acids, a wireless system that controlled boats … All of these projects were created in his laboratory in Madrid and were financed by the government at the time. It seems unbelievable, but many historians will tell you that it was in fact easier to perform research at the beginning of the twentieth century than it is today. Actually, the lack of support of research and development is a huge problem in the advance of sciences. What a shame.

All the contraptions we have seen so far were not designed as "robots" in their respective times. They might have been considered robots, but the word hadn't been invented yet. The first recorded use of the word *robot* was in a play in 1920. These "ingenious machines" were known as automatons. In this play, they used the Czech word *robots*, which meant "servant" and over time came to mean "robot."

In general, all these pseudorobots are predecessors to the appearance of two key inventions in the development of intelligent automatization: vacuum valves and transistors. Both discoveries allow for robots to be built much smaller. Before their invention, if you were to build something with minimal intelligence, it would have to be the size of King Kong.

You are probably wondering how these things could have such an impact on robotics. It is hard to explain how a transistor works, but try to imagine a light switch on a wall, and another light switch across from it. In order to turn on, the light needs both switches to be flipped. Now, imagine there is a third light switch, and when all three are pulsed at the same time, music plays. And then, if you turn on the first switch and the third switch at the same time, the light turns blue. The function of this mechanism is to act as the robot's "brain." It is similar to the function of vacuum valves or an electronic circuit based on transistors, and similarly, a simple computer program.

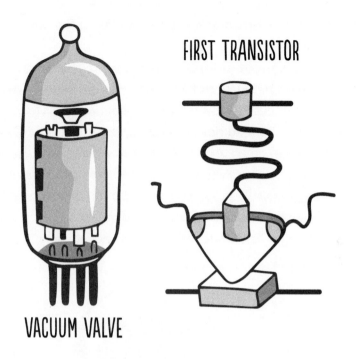

FIRST TRANSISTOR

VACUUM VALVE

If you use only two interrupters, the program will be very simple, but with thousands of these, you can make a calculator or a virtual chess game. Computers and robots have millions of transistors, and these transistors, along with a logic program (software), allow for them to behave as intelligent beings.

We say good-bye to the valves and transistors and continue onward through the history of robotics to the development of robotic arms. These inventions multiplied and spread like mushroom spores during the 1970s. A robotic arm is capable of using tools without human inter-vention and are named "arms" because they look very much like a human arm: they have a fist, a forearm, and a shoulder.

In this era and the years following, there was an increase in production of robots: there were large, reliable machines, but there weren't intelligent programs to control them. For example, the humanoid robot ASIMO at first sight seemed terrific, but in reality, it was very stupid and could do hardly anything; something very simple like ironing a shirt was too complicated for him. Although, when you think about it, does every human know how to iron a shirt? And what's more, do they even like it?

Without Funding, Say Goodbye to Robots

New robots designed by businesses and institutions appear every day. Lots of funding is needed to finalize projects and commercialize these prototypes in the market. Large investments are needed to build commercial robots, while keeping in mind that these prototypes in their early stages are not the best of the best. Because of this, it is common that the first version of a robot is not great, but they also can't improve because their designer had to abandon the project too early because of lack of economic support.

One example of this problem was the poor humanoid robot Robonova, who was created in 2005 and sadly stopped being produced in the following years. They were sold on the market for between $700 and $900. Hardly anyone bought this little toy.

But in 2015, the robot Alpha from UbTech shot onto the market—almost a twin of Robonova—at a price of just $550. Some were for sale online for just $200. The deal of the century!

Check out the evolution of the robot: Robonova had three cables for every servomotor (for every joint); Alpha had one control cable. That is to say, the robot links one motor to the other directly with three cables. This development has a lot of merit, but we aren't going to get into the details right now. Simply put: while Robonova had a single "brain," Alpha has not only one principal "brain" but also a small "brain" in each of its joints. Human beings, in fact, also have these basic functions by connecting the brain to different parts of the nervous system. As you can see, robots get closer and closer to replicating humans.

Humanoid robots, or robots that have the form and mechanical functions of a person, continue to become more affordable. For example, in 2017, the Galician team OP-Robots built a humanoid robot, FrankyBot, and it sold for the low cost of less than $115! How? Using 3D-printed servomotors, which were very cheap to create. You'll be able to make these by the time you finish this book.

Are You a Human or a Robot?

Now you know there are many kinds of robots. One kind that really impresses everyone are logical robots: programs written by human beings that dictate intelligent behavior. One of the most popular is the chatbot, which carries on a conversation with you in a chat and sounds like a human. Other intelligent programs invest in the stock market to earn money, or play *League of Legends* on their own, or assist your character when you're going to make a bad move. These kinds of programs are known as "cheats."

There's an idea that a program could potentially write intelligent programs. Can you imagine? **A program that can create intelligent programs!**

To demonstrate the level of intelligence of a chatbot, we had a conversation with Mitsuku Chatbot, a program available online. We had to talk very clearly because chatbots don't know expressions like *totally rad* or *I'm worn out.*

Me: Hi, Mitsuku.

Mitsuku: Hi, how are you?

Me: Good, thank you, I am writing a book about robots for kids.

Mitsuku: I am happy to hear that. I hope you include me in your book.

Note: Very good response by the robot.

Me: Of course, I can put this conversation in the book.

Mitsuku: That's terrific. Go ahead. Why would you put it in your book?

Note: This second comment did not go very well with the previous, but we continue the conversation.

Me: Because the book is about chatbots and robots.

Mitsuki: I don't believe I have read it.

Me: It has not been published yet.

Mitsuku: Are you sure? I swear it already has been.

(She understands "to publish.")

Note: Here the conversation begins to become a little weird; clearly Mitsuku isn't fully understanding everything.

Me: I am writing it. I need a little more time to finish it.

Mitsuku: Will you include me in your work? It seems like a long time.

Note: Mitsuku isn't exactly Einstein. Why would she combine these phrases? I already told her I would include the chat in the book and also never specified how much time it will take to finish the book. Anyway, we continue chatting.

Me: Okay, I already told you that I would mention you in my book, and I also never told you how much time it would take for me to publish the book.

Mitsuku: What do you think? Do you think anyone would be interested in this?

Me: ?? I hope so, I am putting a lot of time into this book.

Mitsuku: Me too.

Note: At this point, the conversation has become so mixed up that I no longer consider Mitsuku to be "rational." I should sadly say that we have all had more absurd conversations with other people, though.

In summary, in this case, it doesn't seem to us that we could describe Mitsuku as sharp; but nevertheless, with other conversations about simpler topics, her responses can be a little less strange. In fact, she was the winner of the prestigious Loebner Prize in 2016 for being the best chatbot. What an honor for our virtual friend!

2
A CUTE INVASION

As we previously mentioned, many science fiction books and movies have described a world in which everything is controlled by the most villainous machines that want to take power and enslave the human race. We don't believe that this future full of robots would take such a bad turn, nor do we know how it would turn out. What we do know is that these machines have "invaded" our environment, that their numbers grow and grow, and their functions become more varied. What do you think about getting to the point where robots control factories, transportation, and communication?

Robots in the Workplace

The image we have in our minds when we think of the types of machines in factories is a long assembly line with a lot of robotic arms working at once, shooting off sparks and putting things together at supersonic speeds. In some cases, it can be like this, but you have to realize, because of the high cost, pretty much only car manufacturers can have setups like this.

In reality, robotic arms work in what are called "controlled environments," where human presence is practically prohibited. In these places, safety measures detect the presence of people within the work area and automatically stop production if there is a disruption to the normal environment. These extreme safety measures are necessary: sometimes humans are clumsy, and we make bad coworkers with machines. The risk of injury is very high when working with them.

Can you imagine a business where robots and humans working side by side could improve production? And what's more, can you imagine the strange conversations you might have with a machine? "Please, Robot, could you be so kind as to pass me the pliers?" "Yes, certainly, Humanoid, right away." This is a pretty funny scene, right?

However, this robot-helper does not have a reason to exist and it would be more efficient to just do the work of the human itself. Robots are so much more efficient than humans when it comes to completing work: they are faster, more precise, they don't get tired, they don't sleep, and they don't take vacations.

Though it's difficult to guess how it will be, it's clear that, in the future, repetitive work in controlled environments will be executed by machines, simply because they are better than us at this kind of work. Now, in this moment, humans are better than machines at quality control, complex operations, and all the kinds of important work that

requires an expert hand. In some parts of the world, they've already taken note of this and their governments have begun charging taxes for each robot working in a factory.

Robots and Transportation

A few years ago, a well-known online business began a rumor: small helicopters, drones with cargo capacity, would deliver customers' online orders within hours of their purchase. What would it be like when a city was full of swarms of these flying bugs carrying packages everywhere? What madness! People immediately made jokes about all of this.

Some thought that they could capture these with fishing nets and would spend the morning waiting on their roof for drones to come by. Others thought that they could receive their delivery right to their table if they left their window open. Still others were concerned that the drones would drop their deliveries in the middle of the street.

All joking aside, we don't believe that the system was "automatized." But we have to applaud the efforts of the company, their sense of humor, and also their optimism that this would be possible in this day and age.

In reality, the reception and classification of shipments at this point is very much automatized in shipping centers. It is impossible for a group of people to organize by hand all the materials that are shipped or received in a highly productive country such as China, for example. The time it takes to read, process, and sort information is too great.

All the letters and packages are codified, and a swarm of robots take each to their location. Imagine what this kind of place is like: an enclosure the size of a basketball court full of holes in the floor where robots drop their items all at the same time and avoid colliding with other robots. This gives us an idea of the process that follows a package from the time it leaves the vendor, arrives at the post office, and then is delivered to our house. The time in between is minimal, even with international packages.

Robots in Communications

Even the mysterious world of espionage is being taken by robots. Surely, you've seen a movie about spies from the past century where people wearing trench-coats and sunglasses look from side to side while they hide micro-phones in secret places to record conversations and obtain secret information.

They would hide cameras in vases or tap telephone lines. Now, spying is much more sophisticated. You no longer need a team of officials to listen or record images. Well-designed software can do the job. Detection programs analyze phone conversations, selecting phrases, keywords, or whatever dialogue we want. That is to say, these machines are capable of separating the wheat from the chaff and giving us the select information we want.

This legal spy work today is known as big data. This expression refers to the capacity that governments, businesses, and institutions have to create a large database that allows for them to see the data of thousands of people. How they can use this data can seem complicated, but we will try to explain with an example.

The electric energy generated to be used in businesses, homes, and cities is produced in the moment that it is being used. To ensure the supply, energy centers anticipate the peaks of usage. In the morning and in the winter, the consumption of electricity rises like a wave. To keep the electricity from cutting out while we are getting ready in the morning, these companies predict our usage. Robots help us again! Though this sounds unbelievable, a machine analyzes the big data from many areas (weather conditions, day of the week, traffic, highway work, sports results, etc.) and creates a prediction regarding energy consumption. In this way, generators can create the maximum amount of energy in the moment of maximum usage. **Incredible!**

Not every robot is as important as this. There are also much simpler ones that are still very necessary. Here is an example: In times of price wars between telecommunication companies there are a great number of offers for certain things. Someone thought a good way to benefit from this situation is to take the best of each company and create a robot to select the most economic choice. Interesting, right? A robot that helps us save!

These are only some of the examples of how robots can help us. There are so many that we could write a whole other book about robots that help us in our daily life without us even realizing it!

3
CAN YOU WIN AGAINST A ROBOT IN A VIDEO GAME?

Response Time in Bots

Many people hate video games, but you know what? Most of the best information systems and electronic projects have been created precisely for these games. These programmers do crazy things like create programs to beat their own video games. We will explain all this to you with some images from *League of Legends*.

The character (on the next page) on the left is named Nidalee and is throwing a lance to the right. How can the person playing the video game perform this action? They can easily just press a key on the keyboard. What's even cooler is that this player who controls Nidalee is capable of hitting the opposite person in order to win. Yes, the other character is also controlled by a human, and if they are fast with the mouse, they can dodge the lance flying overhead.

Some smarty-pants had the great idea to program a series of lines of code that, when you plug them into *League of Legends*, allow you to dodge almost all enemy attacks while hardly moving a finger. The incredible result is a "dodge-bot" that makes your character dodge a lance headed right toward them.

Who is more intelligent? The human who throws the lance or the dodge-bot who avoids it? Clearly, the player is a human being with a brain capable of thinking of many more things than the dodge-bot. Well, we are in agreement, but is this program terrific or what?

On the other hand, it's also important to realize that human beings take a lot more time to make decisions in critical moments. In this area, computers are much more skilled. As we have seen, a bot can calculate within milliseconds when to dodge the lance. We are not saying you are slow like a snail, but it is certain that you need much more time to do the same thing, probably hundreds of milliseconds.

The community most eager to compare these differences in reactions between people and software bots is the gamers. Take a player of shooting games called Shroud, nicknamed Human Aimbot, as an example. Shroud can position the cursor to aim very accurately and with minimal mistakes. This "machine" has two abilities similar to a robot: reliability, that is to say, if he shoots twice, he hits the target twice; and precision, or the accuracy to hit the object.

In robotics, reliability and precision are very valuable. A robot that walks on its feet, but that curves slightly to the right as he goes, is reliable but not very precise. On the contrary, the same model that walks in a straight line but trips every few feet is precise but not reliable.

Obviously, a robot that walks on his feet in a straight line and doesn't fall is **A MIRACLE!** Excuse me, it is precise and reliable.

Informatics bots are great at making decisions, but they are also reliable and precise. Because of this, it is almost impossible for a human being to beat them, even though it really depends on the quality of the bot, because, clearly, some programs are better than others.

The Decision Trees in *Hearthstone* and *Magic*: *The Gathering*

Since we love to have fun, let's continue playing. Are you familiar with *Hearthstone*? It is a game played with cards, where two people compete with decks of cards and are given specific abilities depending on the selected card.

In the image on the next page, we can observe that one player is dealing a blow of 6 damage to the opponent. In the next turn, the opponent brings an army to return the blow and our champion only has one remaining life point! The game is looking very bad for her ...

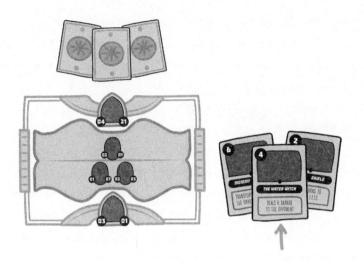

In *Hearthstone,* the speed is not important. Unlike in *League of Legends,* here you can take time to think if you want to take another card from the deck or use an ability to hurt your opponent. We don't have enough neurons to process every single possible outcome. It is hopeless. You will say, "Oh! If you take the dwarf and he has in his hand 'take 2 from everyone,' it leaves me with a clean board and I'm losing. I have to throw the ball of fire so I don't die on the next turn." What a mess...

You see, you decide what you decide from the seven possible actions that you have. After this decision is made, you'll have six or seven decisions that you could make. This is called a "decision tree." Let's do some math, but don't worry, it's pretty easy.

Multiply the 6 possible decisions from the first turn by the 6 possible decisions in the second turn. This equals 36 possible combinations of moves per player in two turns. Keep in mind that the opponent, at the same time, also has all of these options. You see, in one normal game of *Hearthstone* the possible combinations of moves are … hold on … are you ready? Millions!!! The exact number is unknown.

In theory, you could play *Hearthstone* and use a program that gives you recommendations about which cards you should play in each moment, a kind of card-bot or aim-bot for card games. If this program existed, and worked well, it would be based on these decision trees, an informatics technique to decide what to do out of multiple possible options. Humans are much better at cheating these kinds of systems.

The Turing Test

At this point, you must be thinking that machines are awesome. And indeed, they are. There are people like Alan Turing who also believed this, and during the 1950s, he created a test bearing his name. With this test of abilities, this scientific and clever inventor wanted to demonstrate that machines could behave in an intelligent manner, at a level similar or equal to human beings.

In the Turing test, a person sits in a closed room, and a computer is in another. The human can ask what it wants of the computer through a keyboard and screen. If during a reasonable time, they are not able to distinguish whether the being on the other side of the wall is a human or a machine, then, according to this test, the program in this computer has demonstrated intelligence.

This test is used in international competitions, where programmers develop their own chat-bots. The winners of these competitions win great international prestige among the informatics community.

When you are playing a video game and you can't tell if on the other side is a human or a bot that plays the game automatically, you are experiencing the Turing test. When you finally figure out that you're being beaten 20–0 by a computer, then we can say that the Turing test has not been satisfactory because you have discovered that it is a machine.

So, Can You Beat a Machine at a Game?

Of course you can beat a program that plays a video game! You only have to understand its shortcomings. In fact, you already have the advantage and high odds when you play in "one player" mode. In this video game, you can find shortcomings in the program and try to focus on these. This is the case in video games from the 1980s in which you always need a technique to quickly vanquish your enemies. For example, make a couple movements in the same way every time to avoid the rays that the Martians are shooting.

Even though we want to be optimistic, we worry that humans would have a very hard time beating a computer program. Look at Garri Kasparov, one of the greatest chess players of all time. Kasparov played a game of chess against an IBM computer, Deep Blue, and Kasparov won. But, the following year, with a better program, Deep Blue won by a small difference. Many consider 1997, the year this duel took place, to be the year that machines finally vanquished humans. Today, in many games, we can confirm that machines are improving.

Experts who analyzed the chess game that Kasparov played say that the problem is that the computer doesn't get tired and can always play at 100 percent capacity. Some experts think that Kasparov made a couple of mistakes. But in the end, we are all human, right?

4
GREATEST HITS

The Presentation of ASIMO in 2000

The current generation of veteran robotics experts in Spain is made up of people between forty and fifty years old who began using the Internet when it came to Spain in 1995. At this time, their main reference to model robots was the Spring Flamingo from MIT. This robot was a pair of legs attached to a chassis that could turn on a vertical axis and a lateral axis, and could climb and descend small sets of stairs without falling.

The robot was impressive, but its great limitation was precisely that it didn't have good balance and could fall on its side easily. As years passed, other humanoid projects were developed, primarily at MIT and Carnegie Mellon University, but for many, Spring Flamingo was a point of reference . . . until Honda dealt a blow of epic proportions in the year 2000.

In 2000, Honda went public saying it had been working for fourteen years on the creation of a humanoid robot named ASIMO, a friendly robot that could perform basic functions without human intervention. The whole world was amazed, and no one had ever seen the level of quality and detail that ASIMO had; suddenly Spring Flamingo was not the best project.

ASIMO was the result of many evolutions. Honda had begun with a biped robot (only two legs, without a body) that was held with a few harnesses to keep it from falling, and little by little it evolved into the form we know now: a pretty cute humanoid robot with fluid movements.

If you've looked on YouTube, you have probably found some videos of ASIMO falling, where he loses his balance on stairs. In fact, during the first years of his existence, Honda had a contingency plan for when this happened: in a matter of seconds, technicians would place a screen around ASIMO, and he would be swept away out of sight before too many photos and videos could be taken.

Many years after his creation, people started asking when ASIMO would be ready to work in people's homes. The response from Honda was that the burden was no longer on robotics experts, but instead on software developers to develop sufficiently intelligent software, basically avoiding responsibility for developing it further.

DARPA Grand Challenge 2004–2007

The DARPA (Defense Advanced Research Projects Agency) Grand Challenge (DGC) is like a movie script: the United States government gave a million dollars to the team capable of developing a self-driving car the fastest.

Obviously, there were several failed attempts, but in general, the results were very successful, and the competition produced many cars capable of traveling long distances.

At the first competition in 2004, the winner drove 7.5 miles, but none of the cars finished the course so the prize remained unclaimed. Since the competition was considered a success, in 2005, they brought it back, and the best car lasted for seven hours and won the grand prize.

Years later, in 2007, they created a third contest called the DARPA Urban Challenge where the cars had to navigate an urban area (with traffic lights, crosswalks, intersections . . .), much more difficult than the previous contests. Six teams finished the course successfully.

The DGC was a great milestone because many of the people who participated were able to get jobs with businesses that develop these cars. Many cars that were developed at this time got their start in these competitions.

DARPA Robotics Challenge 2012–2015

The DARPA Robotics Challenge (DRC) was a competition for autonomous robots that took place between 2012 and 2015, and that was initially steeped in controversy. The objective of the DRC was for teams to build autonomous robots that looked like humans (though some used wheels instead of feet) and could perform simple tasks like turning on a faucet, opening a door, and cleaning.

You may be saying, "Okay, so what's the controversy? The whole world is on board with this mission," but the problem is that when people say things like "the robot is capable of using human tools," it can be easily interpreted to mean "the robot is capable of using a weapon." Nevertheless, these concerns were put to rest and the DRC was a great success. The robots certainly had a lot of mistakes and it was not a bed of roses, but the developments made were important and had a crucial impact on the perception of the United States in the field of robotics.

Meanwhile, in Europe . . .

While Japan, China, and the United States were hosting competitions, in Europe, they were much more focused on lobbying. That is to say, they were focused on finding sponsorship from businesses and institutions well positioned to provide grants. For example, one program was called H2020 where money is granted to a specific institution in the hopes that they will be successful.

The situation with the Research and Development in Europe is a shame and shows a lack of leadership in the field of robotics.

5
A CHRONOLOGY OF
FAMOUS ROBOTS

Automated Functions in Airplanes

Autopilot in airplanes is a combination of systems that help fly a plane without human intervention in certain functions. This already existed in 1920 and was implemented with simple mechanisms, but at the time it was revolutionary.

Take, for example, the planes used in World War I with machine guns in the propellers. How did they avoid shooting themselves in the propeller? Because there was a simple mechanical system that knew when the propeller passed by the machine gun.

Currently, autopilot systems are much more elaborate than this, allowing planes to fly on predefined routes and managing issues that come up during the flight. Planes can fly pretty much on their own without a lot of risk, but it is important to still have a human team ready in case of an emergency.

Thermomix

Many people say that the Thermomix (or Vitamix) or "kitchen robots" are not robots. Nevertheless, if we say that Vaucanson's Digestive Duck was a robot, or Torres de Quevedo's chess player was a robot, we could say that these appliances operate with a certain pseudo intelligence that allows them to cook like robots.

The Thermomix was created in 1961, and since then it has evolved a lot in its functions and capabilities: heating food, blending, mixing . . . but it is also expensive and noisy. It is interesting that a lot of robotic products go through so many developments, and sometimes the first version has better "public perception" than later versions, even though later ones may be better, like a roller coaster.

Currently, appliances like Thermomix and Vitamix are seen as way too expensive for what they can do, though their owners give the impression of being in a "club." A club where the price of entry is $1,000!

Roomba

A famous modern robot is the Roomba, a vacuum cleaner that has been sold for homes since 2002, costs $300 and cleans the floor while you do other things. You can set the

Roomba to work when no one is home, but legend has it that can be dangerous.

The story goes that a family left their Roomba in their house with their dog and set it to a cleaning program; but while the Roomba is smart, it's not that smart, and it didn't realize that the puppy, who we'll called Poopy, had pooped on the floor of the living room. Along comes Roomba, and since it can't smell or feel anything, it found Poopy's "present" and spread it all over the house.

Roomba is known for getting stuck in corners, under tables, behind curtains, under the kitchen counter . . . so maybe the Roomba in Poopy's family didn't spread the "gift" over the *whole* house. When the mother returned to the house, she told the father over the phone that the house was a war zone . . . with a clear message: "Oh, it's bad, it's very bad. . . . I'll call you back."

Roomba was a huge success and had huge sales. Many people spent whatever they needed to, which at first was about $700. People who are fans of gadgets are known as early adopters. These are people who have no problem spending a lot of money on new products even though the practical thing to do would be to wait until the price comes down. For example, when the PS4 came out, early adopters paid an arm and a leg to say they were the first people to buy it.

Eventually, people hacked their Roombas, to trick them out with colors, sensors, LED lights, spoilers (we're not kidding), and made a business selling these kits to make robotics geeks laugh. The kit was expensive, but it was decent.

Service Robots Wakamaru and Pepper

In 2005, the Japanese company Mitsubishi developed a robot that people called "humanoid/social," which is a nice way to say "it's a humanoid robot that isn't capable of much, but oh well! It moves its hands, moves its head, and that is pretty cool." Obviously, it won't help you clean your house or take you shopping, but at least it can put on a little show.

Wakamaru was a robot for fans of futuristic visions of robots; but obviously, after a few minutes, if not seconds, people lost interest. Years later, in 2014, the French business Aldebaran Robotics debuted a similar robot named Pepper. This robot was created serially and was shown around Europe at robotics fairs and on the news on TV. It was treated like a show. Pepper had a tablet built into its chest so it could interact with the public.

The robot had a program that you could modify and was capable of voice recognition and responding with programmed answers... obviously you could put a chat-bot program into a robot like Pepper, but the chat-bot

can run out of phrases that seem natural. Humans still have to make an effort to believe that robots can behave in sociable ways, and we would have to improve the software and hardware to create a really gratifying experience talking to a robot.

The way Pepper used a tablet is an example of the limitations that intelligent software has: you can put in voice recognition software (a program that recognizes what people say), and voice synthesis (a program that's capable of speech), but if the intelligence of the robot is not elevated, the conversations will be mediocre.

ASIMO

Some very popular robots are not very intelligent; for example, ASIMO, Honda's robot, is a humanoid robot that is very cute but has limited skills. They have spent twenty-five years working on it, and finally the day came when the Japanese developers could take it out and show it to the world and say, "Hey, look, this is only going to work when we have better software."

Today, in 2018, if we list ASIMO's merits, the list would be as follows. He can:

–walk
–walk without falling constantly
–walk with more style
–go down stairs
–dance badly
–dance a little better
–jog

The evolution of robotics is not linear; that is to say, it doesn't progress little by little in a uniform way, but instead goes in spurts, and then all of a sudden, a robot comes out that gets copied by other builders. After they develop a robot that recognizes faces, for example, then others copy the idea; but with these first humanoid robots,

the truth is that they have been built with few milestones. One milestone is a significant advance—think of the discovery of America; this was a great milestone. But the problem with humanoid robotics is that we have a few advances but never a giant milestone.

If you ask certain robotics experts, they will tell you that an important milestone was achieving the ability to jog. A humanoid robot is capable of running simply by separating his legs from the ground for tenths of a second, and this is a very high standard. For you, it's normal—you stand up, take a few strides lifting your foot high, and it feels pretty easy—but for a humanoid robot, this is very complicated.

A human being had to first go through millions of years of evolution to stand on their feet, but our humanoid robots only have about forty years of history. A little jump for a robot puts a ton of stress on its joints, and while they don't feel pain, after time their servomotors (their knees, elbows, ankles) suffer from running. It is difficult for them.

BigDog

If we named a business that has dominated the field in these past years, it would have to be Boston Dynamics, an American business formed by graduates of MIT (the Massachusetts Institute of Technology) that developed many robotics projects in the 1990s and 2000s.

Their best-known robot is a robot dog that you can try to push over but it always stays upright, even if it's walking on ice, where it's slippery. Maybe you've seen videos online.

Years later, WildCat came out, a better version of BigDog. Maybe the coolest thing about these robots is that they use combustibles so that the electricity

consumption peaks aren't a problem. We'll talk about this in another part of the book.

Atlas

This robot is not as well known to the public as the Japanese robot ASIMO, but Atlas played a much more important role between 2013 and 2017. Atlas, a robot created by DARPA in collaboration with Boston Dynamics (the creators of BigDog), was part of an important competition called DARPA Robotics Challenge between different teams during 2012 and 2015.

The DRC ran a series of tests where the teams could personalize their humanoid robots to complete tasks: turn on faucets, use tools, drive a car with their hands, etc. The videos of the tests are online, including a blooper reel with funny music that went viral in 2015.

In an impressive video, we saw Atlas swing between boxes like an acrobat. Until a few months ago, they only worked with quadruped robots, but the engineers at Boston Dynamics had made them able to jump about one meter in height.

Autonomously Functioning Cars

While autopilot functions have existed for decades on airplanes, these programs are still difficult to develop for cars. This is because the routes airplanes fly in the sky are much more spacious, whereas the streets cars drive on are full of obstacles. In general, flying a plane is easy work (even pilots would say so), and a human pilot is only necessary for a small percentage of time to oversee difficult situations.

For vehicles that drive on roads, this is more difficult: from a stoplight turning red to a child chasing a ball into the street, these are life-and-death situations. The machine has to process so many variables at such a fast speed, making autonomous driving very dangerous. Cars have been able to drive on their own for years, but not with reliability, and this reliability needs to be at 99,999%—that is to say, we can't allow for the smallest mistakes. But this is ironic, because so many adults drive with their cellphones in their hands, right?

In the United States, a pretty wacky competition called DARPA Grand Challenge asks participants to modify cars to make them drive autonomously. The first edition of this was in 2004 and the second in 2005 (not to be confused with the DARPA Robotics Challenge); universities, businesses, and research centers modified cars to drive autonomously across a deserted area without leaving the road, without flipping over, and while avoiding obstacles.

Today, we see cars in commercials that drive on their own, that have an autopilot mode for the highway, or that can alert you to if there is something in front of or behind the vehicle. A lot of progress has been made in this area over the past fifteen years, and it is likely that by 2020, we will be talking about self-driving cars as a normal thing, maybe not driving 100% on their own, or not in every country, but it is very likely that by 2025–2030, humans will even be banned from driving in cities, and people who like to drive for fun will have designated places where they can drive as much as you want without risk of pedestrians being in the way.

It could seem that denying humans the right to drive on roads is an assault on their freedom, but when the day comes that robots are more reliable drivers than humans, how could we explain any crashes at the fault of a human driver? This day is coming sooner than we think, and the big car companies all have this mission in mind.

6
MAKERS AND MAGIC

Few things are more fun that building something yourself. Now that we've come to the time to design our robot, we want you to know that you are becoming part of the marvelous and unique community of Makers. Wait, don't close this book! You don't have to sign anything, it is free, and we're not making you take a picture for an ID card that makes you look like a zombie.

What is a Maker? Someone dedicated to creating an object with their own two hands, sometimes in a team, to share with other people afterward. For example, if you break a doorknob, you would go to the hardware store, buy one, and have the locksmith install it. A Maker would print one with a 3D printer and install it themselves. How cool is that?

Everyone is welcome in this world: boys and girls; tall people and short people; smart people; 3D printer fanatics; Star Wars fans; gamers; and well, the list goes on.

THE MAKERS

Before this book was written, there was no Wikipedia entry for "Maker," so we created one. This is very much like a Maker to do; but it was removed a little later because it was not enough of an "encyclopedic" entry, which is very much like Wikipedia to do.

To be a Maker, you need lots of motivation to make things, help other people, experiment, and learn; and to build a robot, you need tons and tons of patience and enthusiasm. It is common that the cables that you're using to create a prototype can have bad connections, and that the robot doesn't work, and that you have to work for hours until it will move. There is nothing more common in robotics than when a robot still doesn't work, even when you think you've done everything. Our advice: patience, patience, patience.

It's annoying: rather than waiting for the robot to work, you wait for it to **NOT WORK** so you can fix it. From here, we get the famous phrase "Finally, it doesn't work!" This mix of patience and enthusiasm is called resilience.

So now, before we build any robots, before we buy any materials, we need to talk about how a robot is not a game of *League of Legends*; robotics does not have moments of instant gratification—it's not like you push a button and the little robot moves. It takes hours or days to build a robot. Resilience is the number one thing we need in order to build a robot, and it is **FREE!**

Certainly, you know someone or you yourself have played at building robots. Maybe with a LEGO kit or with Playmobil, you've felt like you're building a robot. That's a great start, but robotics is more than just building with your hands.

Magic Cables

At this point, you know a lot about robots. Did you realize that? You know that robots and humans move in similar ways. For example, our arms stretch up when we yawn because the brain sends a command that the central system receives and distributes to them.

For now, robots don't do this when they yawn, but the mechanism that makes this movement is keyed into us. A robot has a central chip in place of a brain, and it is wired with electronic circuits instead of a central nervous system. The chip gives the command, the electronic circuit receives it, and the motors perform the function.

DON'T PANIC! We will explain these new words coming up.

An electric circuit is a device made of conductive materials that allow for electricity to circulate through them. A very simple circuit is composed of three AA batteries, an LED lightbulb, a cable, and an interrupter.

And now the magic begins...

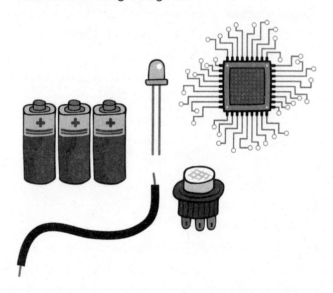

The electric current's path begins in one of the batteries, passes through the cable, and arrives at a stop that absorbs some of the energy to keep the LED from melting; it continues through the conduit, arrives at the interrupter, and returns to the other end of the battery.

An electric circuit conducts electricity, but the electronic circuit is still very cool and allows a robot to activate its motors, sensors, and the chip. If we compare a robot to a human being, the similarities are impressive: the human brain is capable of controlling muscles in the legs with small electric pulses generated by the brain through the nervous system, while the electronic circuit in a robot allows for the small electric pulses from the chip to control larger electric pulses in the motors.

Electronics are the nervous system that control muscles (motors and actuators in general) that the chip controls. The chip that controls the robot can be a micro-controller or a microprocessor. The former has less ability for processing (less ability to do complicated calcula-tions), while the latter has more ability for processing. For example, washing machines have only microcontrollers, while cellphones have a microprocessor, similar to desk-top computers.

The electronic circuit is built on a control board. For instance, in the world of video games, you have graphics cards that have an updated board capable of processing a large amount of graphic elements: houses, cars, the sky, the sun, lights, dirt.... You can get this thanks to a chip called the GPU. The GPU has to have a very good graphics card or else the game won't look good.

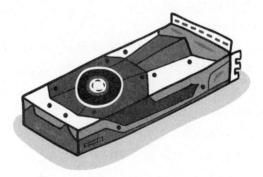

This is the electric circuit for a 1080 GTX graphics card, which cost about $900 when it was for sale in 2017.

Typical robots have less processing capability than a game tower. Game towers are computers with a great capacity to process the newest updates, and cost a fortune. It is interesting that something as silly as video games could be leading fields like electronics.

The explanation is simple: this happens because of the huge amount of money put into this sector. If a small amount of what's invested in improving computer accessories for gaming was dedicated to developing orthopedic prostheses, within years, there would be a huge market for protheses.

Many robotics experts who aren't fans of electronics are not amenable to having to make their own circuit boards. This is not a problem today, because it's easy to buy any accessories for robotics that you need. People who work in electronics will say that it's important to make your own circuit board, but you can trust our advice: electronics are already there, so what the world needs is intelligent software to make robots do what they need to.

Let's begin with the basics: interpreting an electric circuit. It is important to be able to understand electronic circuits and is also very easy.

The first thing is to learn what "electrical potential difference," or "voltage," means. Like we've said, here is some very cool magic, because while we understand how a circuit works, we can't see what happens in it—we can only see the results it generates. If you have a few connected batteries, these batteries have two poles: GND (ground) and 5 volt (or 3V, 3.5V, 6V, depending on the voltage of the batteries). This is called electrical potential difference or voltage.

Sample representations	Definition
	Ground or GND: In electronics, the low voltage (what we will be making) created by the GND can be a pin that generates 0 volts from the battery, which is sometimes called *grounding surface*, that is the whole metallic zone dedicated to the GND.
+22 V	The supply can be represented by the battery icon with two poles, or one thread where the voltage is indicated that shows the thread in relation to the GND. Here you see 22V, which means 22 volts, but in general in robotics, we will use abbreviations like 5V, 9V, and 12V.
4.5 V (3 x AA)	Here we have a combination of ground and battery, which can seem a bit complicated, but it is only to show what we've already talked about. In this case, the supply is formed with three AA batteries (the most common ones that come in toys and everything else) and in total produces 4.5 volts. On one side, the batteries are connected to the GND by your circuit, and it's clear that this diagram doesn't show that the GND is connected to anything else.
	Here is the pulsator or interrupter: a button that you can push with your finger. Here we can see that this circuit closes when you push the button. That is to say, the current passes through the circuit to turn on, for example, a light bulb. When the button is pushed, it closes the circuit and allows the voltage to circulate through.

 Anode Cathode	Electronics often have complicated names, but this is just a lightbulb. LEDs use all their parts and have two sideboards, one called an *anode*, and the other called a *cathode*. The cathode is a negative electron connected to the GND when the current is turned on. LEDs generate cold light, meaning they don't heat up lightbulbs, and because of this they use a lot less energy than other lightbulbs.
1.2kΩ —WW— R6	Resistors limit the passing of the current through the circuit. These are important because some components can't handle the full charge of the current and it will cause them to melt. Resistors keep the current from burning the components.
R + 9 V Green	This circuit is a complete circuit and has a green LED and a resistor to limit the passing of the current and keep the LED from burning and melting the supply (batteries or a wall adaptor) that is 9 volts. If 9 volts go directly to the LED, it will burn, so the resistor is important. Resistors can be different sizes, but those calculations are more advanced than what we are learning in this book.

The circuits that you're looking at are not representations of what we are going to build, but rather they are conceptual and called circuit diagrams. We will look at a protoboard and how you can connect it.

"Protoboard," or Prototype Board

We already know what an electric circuit consists of. Now we will look at a prototype board. One secret: this board is the best friend of a Maker. You will see why.

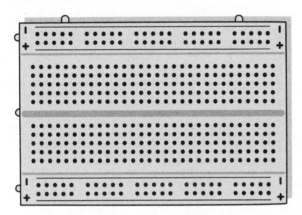

If you look carefully at the drawing, our dear board looks like a beehive. Don't worry, you won't be stung by a swarm of bees. All these little holes are for the cables and electronic components.

The board is one piece inside, so that if you put a cable in one hole, this cable will be connected to all the other ones internally. This makes it possible to make connections between all of them without needing to use a lot of tools.

Heads up: sometimes the cables that we plug into this board can fold a little bit. If they have been used a lot and you see that they've coiled up like a churro, it is better to cut this cable and begin again. Don't worry if you throw out some LEDs or resistors; it is very cheap material. You need to make sure you have good connections, right?

This special hive has two zones: one is the central, where the holes are connected; the other is the side where the holes are separated into different groups. In the second image, you can see this clearly:

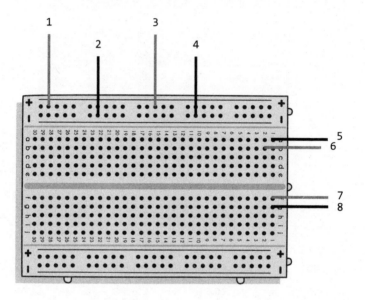

Cables 1 and 3 are joined because they are in the same row; and for the same reason, so are cables 2 and 4. Careful! Pay attention: in the central zone, cable 5 is not connected to cable 6. Cables 7 and 8 are connected, but not connected to 5 because they are in different columns.

The protoboard joins circuit systems. Assembling the two elements is like reading sheet music: at first, it's a bit of a headache, but once you get used to it, it's like reading a comic book!

As you can see, every piece in the diagram has to be connected to the protoboard. As the saying goes, "it's not rocket science," but you have to be careful not to attach the batteries until the end, because you might melt the LED. If your friends come by to ask you to hang out and you run out of the house to meet them, you don't want to leave your circuit connected, right? If you are not there, remove the batteries. This is **VERY IMPØRTANT**.

3D Design At Last!

We've already learned what's going on in the "guts" of our "bug." Now we will design its outside appearance. We may not be able to make it look like your favorite rapper, but we'll try to make it look as cool as possible.

Until recently, building a robot's structure was a total headache. Finding the right pieces was very difficult. You had to buy boring plastic or metal slats and mechanize them, or transform them, as best you could. It was not easy.

Fortunately, 3D printing has arrived! Now making a robot's structure is a piece of cake. With this technique, it's possible to create a three-dimensional model. It could not be easier: you can make your own design on the computer, or download whatever you want from the Internet, and print it on an amazing 3D machine, which is becoming more affordable.

Programming, or How to Talk to Your Robot So It Understands You

Now that you have the electronics and the mechanics, it is time to program the robot. For this, you need to use programming language; for example, the language called C. C is used commonly with robotics, and since it is a little complicated, there are visual tools that help simplify the program.

You might be thinking that you don't know anything about programming, but remember that you are really not going to have to do much programming. You can find everything you are looking for online. Copying code from the Internet isn't always perfect, but taking into account that it is how the vast majority of software companies in the world survive, we can't take it for granted or be picky.

The Energy of the Robots

One of the most important limitations that robots have always had is that they are not energy efficient. Efficiency refers to the ability to adequately complete a function. For example: you have toast and a hot chocolate for breakfast, and then you can go to school, pay attention in class, solve math problems, and play sports. But a robot cannot function for so many consecutive hours, and it can't operate as capably as you. For a humanoid robot to move around like this, or to do a handstand or spin in the air, it is necessary for it to have control of its limbs and also lots of strength, so it needs a very strong and long-lasting battery. Imagine walking with an elastic string tied around your legs: you'd be very tired after a short time. This is what happens to robots.

Lack of efficiency can be resolved with strong sources of energy: gasoline, electricity, compressed air, etc. Remember BigDog? This little dog was fueled with gasoline, and this made him more efficient.

Gasoline isn't great though: it causes lots of pollution and is dangerous and expensive. Electric batteries are a much better option.

7
TIME TO BUILD ROBOTS!

Finally! We are ready to build a robot, step by step, that can perform all the basic functions of robotics: mechanical, electronic, programming, and energy. Can you believe it???

The robot will have a few parts:

- Motors in order to move (like legs)
- Sensors to perceive what's around it (like eyes)
- Control panel (like a brain and central nervous system)

The robot you are going to build is a "free model," which means that the pieces, circuits, and components are available to the public, and then we can modify the robot however we want. Also, there is a video on the Internet that we can watch to see how this is done; all the archives are available to you on the Facebook page of the National Robotics League (https://www.facebook.com/roboticsleague). When using someone else's design, it is always important to give credit to the original author when describing your robot.

There are many other robots that you can make with these beginner programs, but we have chosen one that we believe is easy to build and program.

As we have said, physical robots consist of actuators, sensors, and a brain or unit for processing information. Our robot has the following parts:

Actuators, or exits, that is to say, the devices that allow the robot to communicate or interact with its environment:

- 2 motors
- 3 LEDs (red, yellow, and green)
- 1 RGB LED (this can have many colors)
- 1 small speaker

Sensors, or entrances, that allow the robot to receive information:

- 2 pulsators
- 2 infrared line sensors
- 1 infrared distance sensor

Control unit, that creates the nervous system of the robot:

- Arduino Nano (board base)
- motor driver
- general interrupter

Energy source:

- 350 mAh 2 cell lithium battery

Lithium polymer batteries are often used in the field of radio control, in remote control cars, model planes and helicopters, etc. They have greater capacity than regular batteries, but be careful! They can be charged only with special chargers. And it is important not to charge them too much or it can shorten their working life.

Materials

Now we are going to explain how to build a robot. First, we will make a list of all the materials we need.

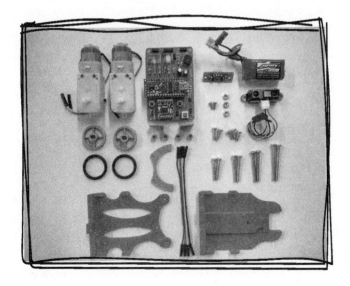

Printed pieces:
- base
- top
- wheel x 2
- front pivot x 2
- back pivot x 2
- bumper

Electronic material:
- control plate
- line sensor plate
- motor x 2
- infrared distance sensor
- strip of 4 female-female cables
- lithium battery

Other materials:
- topic joint x 2 (O-ring gasket)
- M2 x 6 mm screw (2 pcs.)
- M3 x 30 mm screw (2 pcs.)
- M3 x 25 mm screw (2 pcs.)
- M3 x 20 mm screw (2 pcs.)
- M3 x 8 mm screw (3 pcs.)
- M3 x 10 mm (2 pcs.)
- M3 nuts and bolts (3 pcs.)

Step 1: Assemble the Base

We are not going to build this house from the roof down; instead, we are going to start at the bottom of the robot.

1.1. Attach the Motors

Take the printed base and situate the motors as you see in the picture below. To attach the motors, use the M3 x 30 screws, one for each motor.

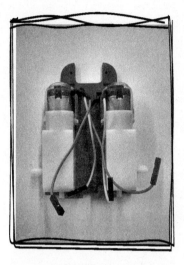
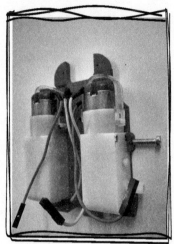

1.2. Attach the Line Sensors

Simply attach the plate and the bumper to the base with the M2 x 6 screws. Careful! The plate should be in contact with the base, and the bumper goes on top of the plate. Pay careful attention to the orientation of the plate.

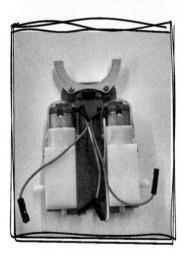

1.3. Put the Battery in Place

Situate the battery between the motors, making sure it is firmly in place.

Step 2. Build the Next Level

2.1. Passing the Cables

You have to pass the cables for the motors and the battery through the openings in the top piece. The cables for the left motor go through the left opening, while the cables for the right motor pass through the right opening.

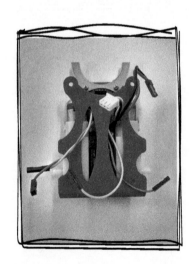

2.2. Anchor the Motors to the Top Piece

Fasten the M3 x 25 screw into the top piece just like you did with the bottom piece. In this case, the screws are held in place by the pressure from the battery. Make sure you don't break the case that protects it. Anchor the back part with the M3 x 20 screws on each side.

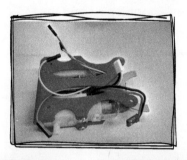

2.3. Wheels

You simply have to put the O-rings around the tires and press them on so they attach fully to the axis of the motor.

Step 3. Attaching the Control Plate

Place the plate on top of the base you have just assembled. See where there are four holes for screws and match them to the plate. The back part is attached with the cylindrical pins and the M3 x 8 screws, while the front part is with the hook-shaped pins and the M3 x 10 screws, with their corresponding nuts.

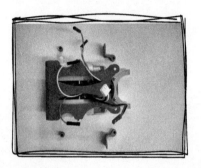

To finish this assembly, you only need the distance sensor. Attach the screw and the nut that you have left over to the sensor with the hook-shaped pins.

Step 4. Connections

You still have a lot of cables. We are going to show you one by one where they attach.

Motors: Connect the two cables from each motor to the corresponding side. Then we are going to make sure the polarity is correct.

Battery: You only have to connect the cable with the red connector. The cables with the white connector are only used for charging. Pay close attention to the polarity of the battery connector. Touch the blue interrupter to the plate and see if it lights up.

Distance Sensor: The three-pin connector connects to the front part at the right side of the plate. Follow the order by color, as shown in the photograph.

Line Sensors: Simply connect the cable between the sensor plate and the control plate without turning it.

Basic Checks

Before starting up your robot, before programming it, you have to make sure that all the sensors and actuators work correctly. Let's begin with the sensors.

We have the line sensors and distance sensors. Both sensors emit infrared light and process reflections. Our eye cannot see this light, so even if the sensor is on, we cannot see it.

Cameras can show infrared light, so let's use a camera to check if it's working. Good idea, right? It's easy: turn on the robot, and then focus your cellphone camera on the sensors. If you see a point of light, the sensor is working. If you can't, then check your connections and try again, making sure nothing is blocking the light.

Now let's check the motors. To see if they are working, let's do a little programming test. If the program is already in place, turn the robot on by pressing the button on the right. The robot should follow this sequence: forward, backward, right turn, left turn, turn clockwise, then turn counterclockwise. If the robot doesn't follow this sequence, you need to check the cables and make sure they're in the right order.

Step 5. Testing the Sensors/Actuators

Now we will perform all the test programs to make sure everything works correctly.

LEDs and Buzzer

If you turn on the robot, the LEDs should follow a specific sequence and then a whistle will blow. Watch the RGB LED and the amount of colors it can produce.

Distance Sensor

If you turn on the robot by pulsing the left button, the robot enters the "valet parking" mode, that is to say, it will blow a whistle when it gets close to an object.

Line Sensors and Motors

If you turn on the robot with both buttons, the robot should follow a dark line drawn on a light surface. You can do this test with a black string. If the robot follows the string, everything is working correctly.

Step 6. Programming

The brain of our robot, or the part that we can program, is a plate called Arduino Nano. Arduino is a system that has revolutionized the world of robotics. Before Arduino, there had been a lack of study and understanding with regard to electronics and programming to construct a simple robot. Despite the simplicity of Arduino's code, you would need a few books like this to begin to give orders to the robot. The instructions are written in a list with a series of keywords that the program translates so the plate can understand.

To simplify this work, there are programs that work from blocks that are easy to understand and that translate our instructions to the right language for Arduino. One of these programs is called Mblock, and we are going to show you how it works.

Mblock is a program based in Scratch, a fantastic tool created to introduce kids to programming. Scratch lets you create stories, videogames, presentations, drawings, etc., simply by putting together pieces of different characteristics. One of the limitations of Scratch is that it only creates computer programs. Here is where the creators of Mblock come in. They joined Scratch and Arduino and brought programming robots to all the boys and girls in the world, since their program is freely distributed!

Step 7. Make it Work!

Ready? Let's go. The first thing that you have to do is download and install Mblock on your computer. There are versions for Windows, Linux, and Mac. All the information about the program can be found at www.mblock.cc.

If you open the program, you can see the panda icon for the project. In our case, we aren't going to use the panda for anything, so we can go ahead and hide it to better see the things we need. Editor → Hide stage layout.

To program our robot with Mblock, we need to say that we use an Arduino Nano plate. Plates → Arduino Nano (atmega 328).

Next, we connect the robot to the computer. The small USB cable plugs into the connector on the Arduino Nano, and large USB to the port in computer. If everything works as it should, our computer will recognize the Arduino Nano plate on our robot. To verify it, we are going to connect both elements. Select Connect → Serial port → COM? In COM?, it shows the communication port that your computer has assigned to the Arduino plate. Just after selecting this option, the header on the program will change and say, "Serial port connected." If it does this, **JUMP UP AND DOWN**, we did it!

The blocks correspond to the basic Arduino instructions that we find in the section "Robots." The first program that we are going to create will make the LED that is on the Arduino Nano blink. This program is called Blink and is the first step for when you're working on an Arduino for the first time.

The first block of these programs that you are going to create will be "Arduino program." To incorporate this into our program, simply drag it to our blank page.

Next add a block "forever" so you can see that this will make the LED blink repeatedly.

Control → forever, and drag the block below to "Arduino program."

Now comes the interesting part that is necessary to make the LED blink. All this:

Turn on the light — wait a second — turn off the light—
wait a second.

The block turns on the lights, translating it as "set the
digital pin 13 to HIGH." We put the value at 13 because
this is the pin that controls the LED.

Wait is simply "control → wait 1 second."

Turn off the LED is translated as "set the digital pin
13 to LOW."

And we return to wait a second.

Once all the blocks are in place, we are able to program the robot, or transfer the instructions from our computer to the microcontroller that controls the robot. Click
on the Arduino program, then open the window with the
translation to the Arduino's language from our block.
Clicking "upload to arduino" begins the transfer of information. First, it'll say "uploading," and in a few seconds it
will say "upload complete." Once the program is trans-
ferred, all the LEDs will blink very quickly.

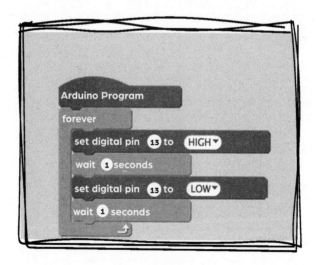

```
Back    Upload to Arduino                              Editar con IDE de Arduino
1 #include <Arduino.h>
2 #include <Wire.h>
3 #include <SoftwareSerial.h>
4
5 double angle_rad = PI/180.0;
6 double angle_deg = 180.0/PI;
7
8 void setup(){
9      pinMode(13,OUTPUT);
10 }
11
12 void loop(){
13     digitalWrite(13,1);
14     _delay(1);
15     digitalWrite(13,0);
16     _delay(1);
17     _loop();
18 }
19
20 void _delay(float seconds){
21     long endTime = millis() + seconds * 1000;
22     while(millis() < endTime)_loop();
23 }
24
25 void _loop(){
```

After installing the program, we have to see the rate that the LED lights are blinking. You can change the rate to make sure you understand the program.

To test all the sensors and actuators on the robot, we have created a series of blocks that can let you give instructions to the robot quickly and directly. You can find all the blocks that we describe below in the section Separate Instructions for Blocks Once the base project is loaded, you can add all the programs here: Archive → Open project → Base.sb2

Separate Instructions for Blocks

Control LEDS:

Color_ON/Color_OFF. Turn on and off the LED green/yellow/red

RGB_Color_ON/RGB_Color_OFF. Turn on and off the red/green/blue LED RGB

Can you tell the difference between the instructions? The first refers to the different colored LEDs, while the second refers to the RGB LED which has red, green, and blue LEDs inside.

Speaker
A beep generates a sound at 400 Hz during a quarter of a second. Basically, it makes a "beep" sound.

Buttons
Release left/right buttons. The program stops until the corresponding button is pressed and released.

Motors
Forward/Back/Right/Left. Move the robot in the specified direction. The number that you put indicates the strength applied to the motors in percentages. For turns, the parameters are related to the turn by how strong and fast the turn is.

Pivot_CW/Pivot_CCW. This turns the wheels of the robot clockwise (CW) or counter-clockwise (CCW).

Stop. Stops the motors.

Sensors
Read line sensors. Read the value of each sensor (right_sensor and left_sensor) and classify them as black or white. This block reads only once and has to be used often if you want to keep reading the sensors (like when you're following a line).

Read distance. This reads the distance when you find an object coming closer (in centimeters) or to keep something at a distance.

Practice Case 1.
Example Program with Basic Blocks

The objective is to reproduce the function of a traffic light. For this, we use the three colored LEDs on the front of the robot. Make sure you put the series of instructions in order, since the robot will execute them without stopping. In case we want to pause, include a pause.

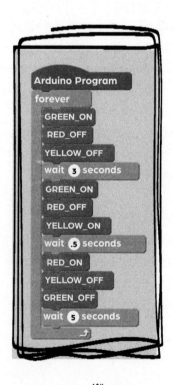

The order of a traffic light is green (3 s)/yellow(.5 s)/ red (5 s).

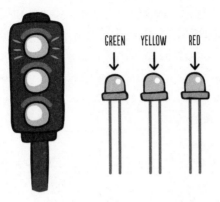

GREEN   YELLOW   RED

Practice Case 2. Follow the Line

This is a simple program, but it is very impressive. The robot follows the line!

First, the robot has to read the line without stopping, and while it reads the lines, the sensors have to choose if it has to go straight (following the line), turn to the right (displaced to the left), or turn left (displaced to the right).

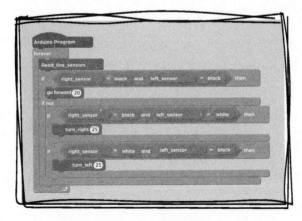

Practice Case 3. Valet Parking

In this example, we will try to reproduce the system of sensors that cars use when they are parking. The basic idea is to read the distance between objects and beep with frequency related to the distance. The key is to realize that we only have to change the time in the pause between beeps.

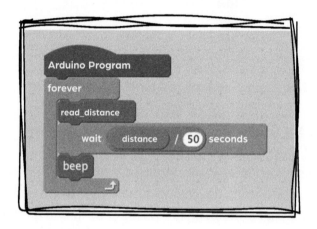

Step 8. Challenges

One of the keys of robotics is the ability to advance and construct complete programs besides the simple bases. With the lessons you've had, are you able to solve these challenges?

- **Rainbow**. Make a rainbow with the RGB light in the middle of the plate. So one second of each color. Begin with cyan and end with red. Can you also make the color white?
- **The Fantastic Car.** During the 1980s, there was a successful fiction series. The protagonist was a robot who "lived" in a black sports car capable of doing tricks (jumps, superspeed, etc.). In the front was a row of LEDs that moved from right to left. Can you reproduce this effect?
- **Barrier in the Road**. This test tricks the sensors. The objective is that the robot follows a black line on a white surface, but it comes across an object in its way and has to continue following the line. Can you get the robot to figure out what to do when it finds an object in the road?
- **Black and White**. You've seen that it is simple to have your robot follow a dark line on a light surface. But what if you change the colors and make it a black surface with a white line? You can also try combining two paths in one quiz: begin with a black line and then change the color of the line. The dif-ficulty of this test is the combination of two simple

blocks. When should you execute each block? The key is to detect the change in surface and direct the flow of the program in conjunction with this.

- **Labyrinth of Lines.** In this test, we are going to make a crazy path and put a wall at the end of the incorrect paths. The objective is to get the robot to follow the right path without running into any obstacles. A little hint: program the robot to follow the outside of the line and not the center. When the robot detects an obstacle, it will turn and follow the same line.

- **Labyrinth of Walls.** Try to build a typical labyrinth, but you can't pass through the walls! First try to see if you can do this with two walls, and then make it a little more complicated. Keep in mind that you can only use the distance sensor and then turn a little at a time to be sure that you can find the open path.

Don't worry if you can't complete these challenges; sometimes there is just one tiny detail that you've missed, and once you realize what it is, **EUREKA!** Another thing you have to understand is that there isn't always only one solution. At the end of the book, you can find one possible solution to these challenges, but it is not the only one. If you solve the challenge with a different program, that's great!

8
IDEAS TO BUILD THE COOLEST ROBOTS YOU CAN IMAGINE

Quadruped and Hexaped Robots

Many robotics experts who have made little self-driving cars are also making robots with lots of servomotors. One of these is called "spider." And yes, it is what you think: robots with feet that can walk. The truth is that they are very easy to make, and they don't require very complicated software, so the spider may not walk well, but it will walk. It is much more difficult, for example, to make humanoids: to balance them or adjust their movements so they stay upright is not easy.

Humanoids

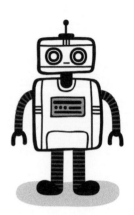

As we've told you, making humanoid robots is difficult. This type of robot is one of the more difficult creations, precisely because each servomotor that you add complicates the robot's balance. In general, the principal limitation is the mechanization, and here we have some ideas: use a humanoid that has simpler joints, like, for example, Zowi, who didn't have knees, or use a humanoid kit that lets you design the smaller joints, so they aren't too loose.

Once it's assembled, the challenge will be to control the servomotors you have: a simple humanoid without knees has 6; a humanoid with knees and ankles has between 8 and 12; and a complete humanoid, with a torso and arms, won't have fewer than 16 servomotors. It is a ton of motors, but fortunately there are plates that control up to 32 servomotors. No problem!

Finally, there's the software; it is a real challenge to control a humanoid in a form that doesn't resemble a FrankyBot. Currently, technology is trying to make sure the movements of these robots are as fluid as possible.

Robots That Imitate Animals

A whole branch of robotics is dedicated to building robots that can replicate characteristics of different kinds of animals. Animal species have millions of years of evolution behind them, and experts study this to see how they've changed and how they've been perfected, and we can learn a lot from them.

For example, have you seen the high-speed AVE train? Its front is shaped like Donald Duck's bill, long and pointed. This is based on ducks' bills because, when they dive into the water, they don't create waves. The designers of this train are very imaginative, and they discovered that when the train enters a tunnel, this design does not create sound waves, keeping the train from being too noisy for neighbors near its route.

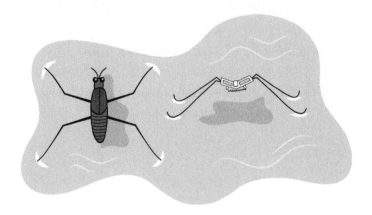

On the right, a robot insect from the University of Seoul that walks on water, to the left, the real insect that it is built after.

Among all the most curious aspects of animals is how high certain insects can jump, like fleas or grasshoppers. A flea can jump **200 TIMES ITS OWN HEIGHT**; that's like a human jumping more than 300 feet straight into the air. This movement can be reproduced with simple actuators if the robot is very light, so that the force of the jump isn't canceled out by the weight of the robot.

Stabilizers on Two Wheels: "Self-Balancing" Robots

There is a special sensor (a device capable of perceiving its environment, like our eyes) called a gyroscope that allows you to know where the robot moves. Imagine if you are juggling and one of the objects is a vertical stick balancing in the palm of your hand, but someone very terrible wants to mess up your skills and tries to move it. You know what? Our brain is very clever and will help you move your hand so that the stick doesn't fall. This is like magic, right? The function your brain performs is based on the top movement of the stick and figures out how to correctly position your hand so the stick doesn't fall.

There are robots that support this principal by navigating without needing four wheels, and they use only two. Surely you've seen the famous Segway on the street. This is a vehicle that drives smoothly, like a Roman gladiator chariot. If you want to change direction, all you have to do is lean the way you want to steer. Though they exist commercially, you can also build your own small "balancing robot."

On the right, a commercial Segway. On the left, a small balancing robot based on an Arduino plate.

Other Ideas

All these ideas we've told you about are well documented on the Internet, but there are also many more topics for you to research and build in your house with the help of the Internet and with our wonderful friend, Patience:

- robotic arm

- robotic hand for sign language

- aquatic robots and submarines

- robots that use solar energy

- robots made from household objects

- robot bird

- self-flying drones

- swarms of robots and collaborative robots

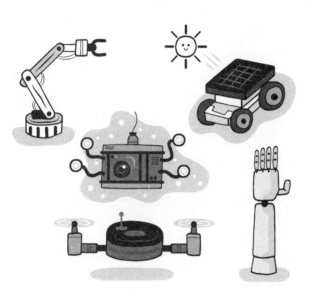

9
JOIN A ROBOT LEAGUE AND AMAZE YOUR FRIENDS!

Yes, Maker, now you know how fun and complicated it is to make a robotic creature. Today there are so many kits for everything, and there are even kits to make the mechanics for our "bugs," and you can buy all the pieces ready-made. If you don't want to do the programming, there are kits where you just need to load the program to the robot, and there are kits for the electronics.

This means that anyone can build a robot: if you prefer programming, then you can buy the mechanics and the electronics ready-made. But if you want to build impressive robots, robots that have a story, then you need to have multiple skills—you need to be able to make the mechanics, electronics, and programming, and also know about human physiology, music, chemistry, aerodynamics. … As you can see, studying a lot is **IMPORTANT.**

Because of the great interest in specializing robots, in 2008 the National Robotics Competition League, or the League of Robots, as it is known around the world, was formed. The objective of the league is to promote the creation of professional teams of builders who develop their own robots and compete against each other throughout the year to find who is the best team.

At first, the teams were formed by builders who were participating individually. After time passed, more and more teams were formed based around everybody's skills and what their strengths were that they could contribute to the group.

Today it is super important to focus on a specialty rather than try to be a "jack of all trades," unless you are Xavi Puigmal, a builder on the Smith team that won the League of Robots four years in a row, without ever having another builder on his team! These days, the teams are organized in simple ways.

ELECTRONICS

MECHANICS

CHEMISTRY

PROGRAMMING

MUSIC

AERODYNAMICS

To win the League of Robots is the greatest prize you can win in a robotics competition in Spain. There are various requirements to be able to compete in the professional division (PRO division), but the most important requirement of all is to have amazing robots. These are robots you can't buy in the store; you need to design them, build them, and perfect them all on your own.

Many teams have competed in the league with the intention of winning and have fallen short due to lack of knowledge or dedication. It is common for us to have small shortcomings in mechanics, electronics, or programming, but if you have a multidisciplinary team, you work hard, and you learn from your mistakes, you shouldn't have a hard time ascending in the ranks.

Build Your Team

The League of Robots has a series of requirements for new teams: you need to have a name, a logo, a written description of who you are and what you will do, and of course, your robot. Professionals often have robots in every category, but for students, it is much simpler.

For example, you can make a line-following robot and compete in this category, or you can make a mini-sumo robot (robots that wrestle) and compete with other mini-sumo robots. There are fewer requirements for students to enter the competition, but the prizes are also smaller than in the professional division.

NOTE: Your teammates are very important. The team needs to have a specialist for every area. A good working environment is important as well. It is important to get along and have fun, just as much as it is to work hard.

MECHBOTTEAM

Perfecting the Robots

Do you know what the top issue is that competitors encounter in these competitions? Robots that work at home and then don't work at the competition. What a shame! This can happen when the cables on the plate come loose in transport.

When this happens, you might be disappointed, but you have to keep your chin up and fix the problem. It's important to double-check everything, make sure all the wheels are tight enough and the batteries are secure—all these little things can make a big difference as to whether the robot will work.

For robots with wheels, the reliability is important, but for robots with feet that have to walk, reliability is critical. If any of its joints are loose, the robot could fall easily.

For example, a mini-sumo doesn't have to be very reliable, but it has to be able to knock down its opponent and avoid being the robot that hits the mat.

Travel to Japan with Your Robots

We are going to imagine that we've won the League of Robots. So now what? We have to go to Japan! In Japan, they have two of the most important competitions in the world: ROBO-ONE and the All-Japan Robot-Sumo Tournament.

ROBO-ONE is a competition for humanoid robots where they perform a variety of ability tests and one fighting test. The All-Japan Robot-Sumo Tournament is simply sumo on wheels on a metallic surface; the robots have magnets that help them maintain traction and grip the mat.

In Europe, there are more competitions, like the RoboChallenge and the Baltic. But they aren't celebrated as much as the ones in Japan. There are also traveling competitions like the RoboCup, which is held in a different country every year. The problem is that it costs a lot of money to participate in this one, for professionals and for students.

10
FUTURE, ARE YOU COMING?

The field of robotics always looks to the future. Those who work in this field never stop dreaming of what they will build in the coming years.

In this chapter, we will talk about what is coming in the near future, and what we want you to take away from what you've read here, because all of this is happening quickly. It is also important to pay attention to news coming out on social media and try to avoid any scams. Scams include projects that promise great results but are not actually real.

In the next section, we will talk about projects that have been successful, others that seem like scams, and some that actually are scams. The future of robotics will be full of surprises.

We have to be especially careful with crowdfunded projects, in which people like you or me, anyone in the community, can economically support projects. The problem is that some of these projects promise things that cannot be achieved, and it would be a shame to spend your money on these projects only to find that they produce something very different than they initially promised.

THE FUTURE, JUST LIKE THE PAST AND THE PRESENT, REQUIRES A BIG DOSE OF COMMON SENSE.

Haptic Suits and Rigs: Virtual Reality for Your House

A haptic suit is basically a set of accessories you attach to your body that allows you to control a device and feel what is happening as if you were a character in a video game. Do you like this idea? Imagine that you were playing a video game, not using your Playstation controller, but rather a haptic suit, and thanks to this, when you move, your character moves just like you!

This little suit contains small motors and different types of sensors that can cause a physical reaction when, for example, you are pushed in the game, or when the car you're driving crashes. The haptic suit can detect what you're doing and also react before it happens in the video game.

Commercial haptic suits have been developed, and are, of course, incredibly expensive. You could, if you wanted, make your own. The first ones were developed a few decades ago, but the more recent models have greatly improved the quality of the interaction. Let's show you a few examples.

TGV 2011

In 2011 at the University of Pennsylvania, a few students, with the financial support of their professor, developed a prototype for a haptic suit with sensors and actuators.

The sensors they used, like those in any haptic suit, can detect the position of the user, and the actuators help make the user "feel." For example, it is common to use solenoids, which are like small "electric billiard cues," that gently hit the user to simulate the impact of a ball or a punch. This obviously won't injure the user and creates only low–potency impacts.

KOR–FX

KOR–FX is one of the projects that came out as a commercial project. In the moment that this book is written (December 2017), the suit costs $100, a very low price, even though it isn't really a huge thing.

One of the criticisms written about the suit is that it's "like a rumble pack for the body," since the most simple thing to simulate in the suit is a vibration from the console. This effect comes from tiny motors that have an axis divided in the middle, and they turn so they can vibrate all over the suit.

The true achievement of the haptic suits is that they can detect all the movements in the body, and at the same time simulate all the possible sensations of the virtual environment. But is a vibration in the chest comparable to a car crash? Is a vibration in the chest comparable to receiving a kick to the shin? Obviously, it is not the same, and so people were frustrated to have spent the money on something that doesn't have a great user experience. It perhaps would have been better if they'd waited until technology was more advanced.

Teslasuit

The Teslasuit is a suit that, in theory, was going to be commercialized in 2017, but there is no hint of it. In fact, many projects from Kickstarter (a fundraising platform for creative projects) have been flops or scams— there have never been commercial versions of their products for the simple reason that they promised more than they were able to achieve.

Haptic suits can also be used with other robots. For example, you could put on your haptic suit and you'd control a robot that could have a different physical representation than your own. Now we are going to explain to you what a "physical avatar" is.

Physical Avatars

A physical avatar is a robot that you control with a remote control, either a manual control or a haptic suit. Maybe you've seen games like Habbo Hotel or The Sims online, in which a virtual person can be represented in a more or less realistic way.

Physical avatars are still limited in part by the theme of haptic suits; it is difficult to control a humanoid robot with a video game controller, so until a truly reliable haptic suit is developed, it won't be very easy to control a robot that moves around in the real world.

We are familiar with physical avatars from the movie Avatar, in which biological people are controlled by a rig. In the present day, we are gazillions of years away from this happening.

In the movie Avatar, the screenwriters created an easy solution to represent the remote control. Instead of designing a platform where the operator of the avatar had to move controls directly, the movie took place in a universe in which the technology existed so that the avatar could be controlled by a brain sleeping in a bed.

In reality, physical avatars are robots with wheels and arms, with a remote control, and a console that looks like a video game console. These are the type of robots used, for example, to deactivate bombs. Look at the horrible accident at the Fukushima nuclear center. One of the robots they used to go into the area of the melted reactor experienced such bad radiation that the video camera melted, and the remote operators had to take it out of the quarantine zone right away.

It is interesting that when important businesses are prototyping robots for dangerous environments, like nuclear disasters, first level of the DARPA competition, chemical accidents, or natural disasters, they look to simple elements: video game consoles, laptop computers, commercial virtual reality (VR) glasses. While the industry has unlimited resources to develop robots, the only thing they're missing are qualified people with free time and the budget to apply these resources to the creation of amazing robots.

Authentic eSports

For those of us who are dedicated to robotics and information, we couldn't be more excited to hear that some video game players are being considered "athletes" and there is a new phenomenon called eSports. eSports doesn't exactly refer to all videogames, but instead is about "electronic sports," which requires great reflexes and intelligence.

Participants in eSports teams certainly don't use the same kind of physical athleticism, and it is mostly a sedentary activity. We live in a time where obesity is growing, and we should be making sure we get plenty of exercise.

Because of this, VR rigs have been improving to create eSports experiences where you are actually playing a sport. It's impressive to watch someone play *League of Legends* with a lot of skill, but how much effort does it really take to run two miles in the video game? Sports need to require complete physical activity, not just good reflexes in your fingers and hands.

Physical activity or exercise, performing a test with or without a competition, shows ability and strength.

Can the definition of "sport" leave behind physical activity, and include being seated and just clicking really fast? Is someone working in an office playing a sport? This doesn't make sense.

A haptic suit associated with a static platform to simulate a virtual reality environment is called a "rig." VR platforms are very popular, and perhaps you've seen them in some shopping malls and stores. We recommend that before you think they are so cool, you try it out a few times, because many VR systems leave much to be desired.

A VR Platform

The VR platform, in theory, should simulate real movement like a human running. If you look at the picture on the next page, you'll see a treadmill where the user will be walking in place, which is not a particularly nice experience, especially before you get used to the difference in how the simulated movement feels versus running outside. Many people find that these machines never feel totally natural.

Omnidirectional Treadmill

The VR platform that's probably closest to reality nowadays is the omnidirectional treadmill, which allows you to walk in different directions. What's clear is that

To the left, a traditional treadmill; on the right,
a prototype of an omnidirectional treadmill.

omnidirectional treadmills aren't very reliable and most we've seen make it hard for the user to stay in the center, especially when they change the rhythm of the steps.

Infinadeck's omnidirectional belt is advertised on YouTube as the "new" Infinadeck. The comments on this video range from "is it just me or is this a really unnatural way to walk?" to "as long as this looks like it'll make people super dizzy, I won't have this in my house."

Exoskeletons

Exoskeletons are similar to haptic suits, as they also have a lot of sensors, but instead of being simply a cloth suit, they have joints and limbs that "accompany" the movement of the human. We have seen them in movies like *Alien* (the original), *Elysium*, *Edge of Tomorrow*, and *Iron Man*.

These movies show exoskeletons used in ways very different from how they are used in real life. For example, in the movies, exoskeletons are used as prototypes for people with physical disabilities, like paralysis in their legs. These exoskeletons are not very agile or reliable. They are, frankly, a pain. Technology is not yet at the point where a person who can't walk could use this to get around. The money and lack of organization are reasons why these developments haven't happened yet: no business has tackled this because the number of units that would be sold are very few, and it wouldn't pay back their investment.

For example, the movement e-Nable (a community of volunteers who develop protheses for people with amputations and problems with their arms or hands) would be ideal to advance an exoskeleton project, but the use of metal and plastic materials is always a limitation: 3D printing with resin is easier to do than with aluminum, for example.

There are some projects that try to commercialize a metal additive powder to make your own metal pieces at home. It is probable that this could come to fruition in the next few years, even though it isn't easy to do right now. There are still tons of hours of work to do in terms of design and testing prototypes.

In general, exoskeletons that you see in real life can help carry cargo and have a lot of load capacity but not a lot of time before they need to recharge.

Writing this book has gone very well; we have learned so many things, and have so many questions. The most important questions are: Will robots eventually take over every job? Will humans have nothing but free time?

It is difficult to know exactly where the world is going in terms of robots and robotized work, but we are sure there will be tons of robots in factories and all over the place.

We are crossing our fingers that it will be this way, that you will be able to design amazing robots that help people and that we can build a better world.

GLOSSARY

Actuators: Devices that allow a robot to act in its environment.

Aim-bot/cheat: Informatics program that automatizes some of the work that a human player could do to improve the results.

Arduino: The Arduino plate is very useful because it is small and affordable.

CGI (Computer Generated Imagery): Computer design techniques used to simulate real scenes or visual effects, commonly used in movies.

Chat-bot: Informatics program that maintains conversations with human beings, more or less successfully.

Control plate: This plate is where you can find the electronics, mainly the microprocessor.

DARPA: The Defense Advanced Research Projects Agency, a United States organization that launches research and development projects, is open to the public, and has concrete objectives that can be clearly measured.

Hardware Robot: A physical machine that performs functions autonomously, or that simulates intelligence.

Humanoid Robot: A robot that has the appearance of a human being, with legs, arms, torso, and head.

Informatics program: Lines of code that, when executed, define the robot's behavior.

Infrared sensor: A sensor that uses infrared light (light that is not visible to the human eye) to detect obstacles or objects close to the robot, like black lines or walls.

LED: Electric device that emits light when a current runs through it.

LED RGB: An LED capable of showing different colors.

mblock: Visual programming language that helps connect the Arduino plate to the robot by using Scratch.

Microprocessor: Brain of the robot, where the informatics program can execute instructions.

O-ring: A rubber ring used to seal tubes to keep water from leaking and help wheels keep traction.

Robot: In general, an automaton that can perform functions autonomously.

Scratch: Visual programming environment to introduce children to programming.

Sensors: Devices that allow a robot to detect what is happening in its environment.

Transistor: An electronic component that is super-hyper-mega small that, when combined with other thousands or millions of transistors, can make a computer.

Virtual Robot: A software program that performs functions autonomously and simulates intelligence.

DESIGNING YOUR OWN ROBOT

1. What will it do? Think of a situation in which it would be nice to have a robot to help you, and make a list of the characteristics it will have.

....

....

....

....

....

....

....

....

....

....

....

....

ii. What helpful things does your robot have? Decide what your robot needs (lots of eyes, extra arms . . .)

....

....

....

....

....

....

....

....

....

....

....

iii. What is your robot's energy source?

....

....

....

....

....

....

....

....

....

....

....

....

iv. Draw it here!

v. Robots don't have emotions, and so they don't get lonely. Nevertheless, this robot would have more fun if he had a friend to share the work with. Think of other tasks that his friend could do.

....

....

....

....

....

....

....

....

....

vi. What helpful things does this new robot have?

....

....

....

....

....

....

....

....

....

....

....

vii. What is this robot's energy source?

....

....

....

....

....

....

....

....

....

....

....

....

viii. Draw it here!

NOTES

....
....
....
....
....
....
....
....
....
....
....
....
....
....
....
....
....